This belongs to

____

Sharks and Tuna - sharks are group of cartilaginous fish with streamlined bodies, sharp teeth, and powerful jaws. some species are endangered due to overfishing and habitat destruction.
Tuna- are large, fast-swimming fish. They are consumed as fish worldwide. Some species are threatened by overfishing, which has led to strict regulations on their catch in some areas.

Sea turtles - are large, shelled reptiles known for their distinctive flippers and ability to migrate long distances. They are endangered due to habitat loss, pollution, and overfishing.

Jelly fish - are free-swimming bell-shaped invertebrates with trailing tentacles that they use to capture prey. They have a gelatinous translucent body.

Starfish - is a marine invertebrate with radial symmetry and multiple arms. Starfish have a unique ability to regenerate lost arms.

Sea anemone - is a predatory marine animal that resembles a flower with a tube-like body and tentacles surrounding a central mouth.

Sting rays - are cartilaginous fish that have flattened bodies and elongated tails with barbs or stingers.

Seal - is a marine mammal with a streamlined body, flipper-like limbs. they are playful and have ability to swim and dive at great depths.

Dolphin - is a highly intelligent and social marine mammal with a streamlined body, a beak-like snout. it's known for its acrobatic abilities, communication skills, and playful behavior.

Seahorse - is a small, upright-swimming fish with a horse-like head, a curled tail, and a unique way of reproducing where the male carries the eggs in a pouch until they hatch.

Octopus - is a highly intelligent and adaptable mollusk with eight arms. they are known for their ability to change color and shape to blend in with their surroundings, as well as their impressive problem-solving skills.

Snail - snails are gastropod mollusks. They have a unique reproductive system, with many species being hermaphrodites and able to self-fertilize.

Lobster - is a crustacean with a hard exoskeleton, two large claws, a long tail, and ten legs. It's used as a popular seafood delicacy.

Shrimp - are small crustaceans with a long curved body and a fan-like tail. They are popular seafood option worldwide.

Seal

Different species of fish.

Manta rays - are large, filter-feeding marine animals with broad pectoral fins. They feed on plankton and are under threat from overfishing, habitat destruction and climate change.

Sea otters - are marine mammals known for their thick fur, which keeps them warm in cold water, and their use of tools, such as rocks to crack open shellfish. They are keystone species, helping to maintain the health of kelp forests. They are threatened by pollution, oil spills and habitat loss.

Barracuda - are predatory fish that can grow up to 6 feet long and are known for their incredible speed and agility in the water, making them effective hunters. Their sharp teeth and powerful jaws make them potential danger to humans.

Seashells - are hard protective outer coverings of marine mollusks, often with intricate patterns and shapes, commonly found on beaches.

Coral reefs and various species of fish.
Coral reefs are diverse underwater ecosystems composed of living coral colonies and other organisms, and are often referred to as "rainforests of the sea" due to their high biodiversity and ecological importance.

Crabs - are crustaceans with a hard exoskeleton, two claws and legs and are known for their ability to scuttle sideways. Crabs are an important source food to many people around the world.

Shipwrecks and caves.

Angry Shark

Ocean floor, rocks, seaweed, and starfish.

Whale - Whales are large marine mammals that are known for their size, intelligence, and unique vocalizations. They range from the small dwarf sperm whale to the massive blue whale, the largest animal on earth.